Basketball Tips:
Bite-Size Techniques to Boost Your Game

Ed Tennyson

Basketball Tips: Bite-Size Techniques To Boost Your Game

ISBN-13:978-1463541491

ISBN-10:146354149X

PART 1
How to Play
Basketball Better

To enthusiasts, basketball is not just a sport - it is a lifestyle.

That's why they are always on the lookout for ways of improving their skills in the game.

If you are one of these basketball enthusiasts constantly looking to improve your game, then you'll surely appreciate the fact that improving your basketball skills also keeps you healthy in more ways than one.

It strengthens your heart and lungs, and enhances their functions at the same time.

Improving your basketball skills is, in fact, a great way to stay in shape.

It's a good thing, then, that modern technology has made it a lot easier for you to learn the game and improve your skills in it.

Literature, for one thing, is very helpful in improving your performance in basketball.

Whether you're a player, a coach, or simply a fan, you can learn a lot about the sport in publications.

Among other things, literature can teach you how to strategize, how to get into the right shape for basketball, and how to play effective offense and defense.

That's because a lot of basketball experts have put their expertise into print, so now you can learn everything from the basics of the game to the most up-to-date basketball techniques simply by reading up on the subject.

Videos are a great tool for learning how to play basketball better.

After all, there's nothing like seeing how the moves and plays are done for you.

Instructional videos help you work on the details of basketball techniques, from ball handling to passing to shooting and scoring.

You can choose from hundreds of basketball video clips and tutorials on popular video hosting sites like YouTube.

Of course, the best way to improve your basketball game is still to actually go out on the court and play.

No matter how much you read up on the subject or how many hours you spend watching basketball videos, nothing beats the real thing when it comes to learning how to play basketball better.

You should keep practicing all the fundamental basketball skills – dribbling, lay-ups, jump shots, rebounds, and all other skills.

As with any other thing in this world, practice still makes perfect!

When you practice your basketball skills, you may want to invite family and friends to practice with you.

This way, not only will practice be a learning experience for you, but it will also be a fun and enjoyable bonding experience.

After all, no one ever said training for a sport has to be a serious and boring occasion.

There are lots of ways to seriously improve your craft while still having fun in the process.

Above all, always remember that learning how to play basketball and improving your skills in the sport doesn't happen overnight.

Just like any other sport, playing good basketball takes a lot of discipline and commitment.

So, don't be discouraged if you don't achieve your desired results immediately.

Just keep working and you are sure to see these results in time.

Again – practice makes perfect!

And just as you should always keep your body fit for basketball, you should also make sure that you keep yourself healthy by eating the right foods in the right amounts, by getting enough rest, and by pacing yourself well.

Keep in mind that basketball isn't just a sport; it's a lifestyle.

Part 2
Fundamental Skills
You Should Know

If you want to play basketball better, then you most definitely have to understand and master the basics of this game.

This means you'll have to study and practice all six fundamental basketball skills, namely:

- **Dribbling**

- **Passing**

- **Shooting**

- **Rebounding**

- **Offense**

- **Defense**

When you train for basketball, you should concentrate on each of these skills to make sure you can perform well in an actual game.

Dribbling

This fundamental basketball skill is very important because it is the primary way of moving the ball around, particularly when passing isn't a better option and there's no lane available for a clean shot.

Take note that even experienced players often make the mistake of dribbling even when it isn't necessary.

Any professional basketball coach will tell you that dribbling should only be done when it fulfils a purpose.

A very common way for players to lose the ball is when they dribble it while looking for an offensive option.

Remember that no matter how good you are at dribbling, your opponent will always have a better chance at a steal while you're dribbling the ball.

A better strategy to use while looking for an offensive option would be to grip the ball firmly and then position your body between the ball and your defender.

Passing

This is actually the top option for moving the ball around on offense.

It is quicker than dribbling, which means it gets the ball to the open man as soon as possible so he can take the shot.

Remember that most offensive plays are set up by great passes, so working on your passing skills is definitely a good way of improving not only your performance, but that of your team as well.

Shooting

This is perhaps the most practiced basketball skill by any player.

In spite of that, many players still practice it the wrong way.

To truly improve your shooting skills, you should always perform shooting drills at game speed and in the same way you would when under pressure.

Most players do hop-shots during drills instead of the jump shots they constantly turn to during an actual game.

Instead of jumping or power, many players generate power from their arms during practice.

Take note that when you practice the wrong way, you get used to the wrong way of doing things.

So now you understand why you're always missing your jumps shots during the game.

Rebounding
This skill can be used both for offense and defense.

A common mistake is for a player to think that rebounding should be relegated only to the big men.

But, good rebounding takes more than just size.

It even requires more than just jumping ability.

Rather, good rebounding requires skill and dedication.

Skill involves the ability to read the shots and position yourself accordingly.

But, perhaps the most important factor is dedication because the one who is willing to do whatever it takes is usually the one who gets the ball.

Offense
This fundamental skill encompasses all aspects of the offensive court.

Shooting plays a large part in offense, of course.

But, moving off the ball to give options to the one holding it is also an essential offensive skill you need to learn.

Knowing how and when to support your teammates with screens and the ability to find the best offensive option is just as important, but these skills are often overlooked during practice.

Make sure you don't make the same mistake.

Defense

You may have noticed that the best defensive teams in the NBA are often the ones who eventually make it into the playoffs.

From this, it may be safe to conclude that a good defense is the key to basketball victory.

And when you practice your defense, remember that it isn't all about getting steals, or blocking the opponent's shots.

Good defense is, above all, about intimidation.

PART 3
Improve Your Game by Increasing Your Jump Height

For a basketball player, the ability to jump high is an essential skill that's sure to help you bring your game to the next level.

The problem is that there are just some people who find it a bit difficult to jump high.

If you're one of these people, well, I've got good news for you:

Jumping higher is all about technique and physical conditioning.

Even if you're just of average height, you can still jump high enough to dunk that ball, as long as you get the basics right.

Always remember that jumping higher requires you to put more power on the ground.

As the basic law of force says:

"For every action, there is an equal and opposite reaction."

Therefore, you'll have to learn how you can push the ground harder such that it pushes you back up in the air higher as well.

Warming Up

It's a good idea to begin your practice or game with about ten minutes of light jogging.

Take note that properly warmed up legs not only add 2-4 inches to your jump height, but they also reduce your chances of getting injured during the game.

After your jog, try to touch the rim and see just how high you can get.

Continue warming up for 15 minutes and then try again.

You'll be pleasantly surprised at the improvement.

Bracing Before the Jump

Try to stiffen your body just before you make the jump.

The simple logic behind this advice is that the stiffer your body is, the harder you'll push against the ground.

This is a basic truth that many players unfortunately take for granted.

Getting the Right Shoes

It's best to get shoes that are snug, but not too tight; they should feel like an extension of your feet.

You should also remember to lace your shoes up tight.

Again, there's a simple logic behind this advice: Loose-fitting shoes impair your ability to put power on the ground when you jump.

Holding Your Breath

When you hold your breath just before you jump, you're actually adding to your body's stiffness.

And as you already know by now, you're better able to push against the ground harder if your body is stiff.

Focusing on Your Legs

Needless to say, your leg muscles play the largest role in improving your jump height.

Contrary to what you might believe, however, running or jogging doesn't help you build your leg muscles.

Those exercises help increase your stamina, but they also break your leg muscles down.

The best exercises for building your leg muscles are actually squats and dead lifts.

What's even better is that they help your entire body grow because growth hormones are naturally released when you do them.

Take note, however, that you have to follow correct technique in order to avoid injury when performing these exercises.

It's best to take instruction from a professional and do warm-up exercises before these two.

Now, you can start working on the basics of improving your jump height.

But, remember that there's a lot more for you to learn in order to truly optimize your jumping ability.

The good news is that there are lots of programs designed to help you with your jump height and with careful selection, you're sure to find the program that suits your needs best.

Part 4
Exercises to Help You Jump Higher

Every basketball player dreams of being able to dunk.

Well, if you want to accomplish this feat, you'll naturally need to be able to jump higher.

And to jump higher, you'll need some base of strength.

Therefore, the best thing you can do to improve your jumping and dunking skills is perhaps to work out your lower body.

Fortunately, there are lots of exercises you can perform to achieve this purpose.

But, among those exercises, the best ones that'll help you increase you jump height are squats, lunges, calf raises, dead lifts and abdominal exercises.

Squats

This exercise is useful because it works nearly all of your lower body muscles.

Your hamstrings, calves, and abdominals are the fundamental muscle groups that are used for jumping and running, which is why it's important to strengthen them by doing squats.

Take note that you can only take full benefit of squats when you do them in correct form.

In fact, there's absolutely no point in doing squats unless you do them in proper form because you won't be able to work the essential muscle groups when you do squats in poor form.

Lunges

This exercise is great for working your hamstrings, which is very important because it is the primary muscle that provides power to your legs.

Remember that your hamstrings are prone to injury, which makes it even more important to do strengthening exercises like lunges and hamstring curls.

These exercises not only improve your jumping ability, but protect you from injuries as well.

Calf Raises

These exercises work on your calf muscles, which is very important for increased jump height.

Calf raises strengthen not only your calves, but also your toes.

And when you observe a person jumping, you'll notice that his toes are the last parts of his body that leave the ground.

Your toes, therefore, are what propel you into the air when you jump.

This makes calf raises even more beneficial because they help increase your vertical jump by strengthening your toes.

Dead lifts

This exercise is a compound movement that strengthens both the large muscles in your legs and your core.

Furthermore, this exercise triggers growth hormones, which means that it can also help build the muscles in other parts of your body, thus increasing overall strength.

As long as you do this exercise with proper form, you'll be able to utilize the strength of your legs while avoiding possible back injuries when you jump.

Abs Exercises

These exercises may actually be the most beneficial where jumping and dunking are concerned.

When you jump, you create energy from your core and allow that energy to travel to your lower extremities.

This is called kinetic linking.

And when your core muscles are weak, energy is lost during travel.

This is why it is very important to strengthen your abs if you want to increase your jump height and enhance your dunking ability.

These are just some of the exercises that can help you improve your jumping and dunking skills as a basketball player.

They are considered to be the most beneficial, so it's a good idea to make them the focus of your workout session for increased vertical.

You may, of course, complement them with other exercises that can optimize your jumping ability.

PART 5
How to Improve Your Slam Dunking Ability

The ability to deliver a slam dunk is one of the most sought-after skills in basketball.

That's because a slam dunk instantly displays your expertise and establishes your authority as a basketball player.

In fact, a variety of exhibitions and competitions that revolve around dunking have been created over the years.

These exhibitions and slam dunking competitions have continued to inspire professional athletes, aspiring basketball players, and viewers alike.

Take note, however, that while top-calibre athletes make slam dunking look very easy, it certainly is far from being easy.

In fact, it is perhaps one of the most complex of basketball skills.

You must possess a wide range of capabilities and perfect a number of skills and techniques in order to accomplish a successful slam dunk.

The good news is that just like any other skill, constant and dedicated practice will allow you to someday impress onlookers and fellow athletes with your dunking skills.

Effective dunking requires three aspects, namely:

1. Approach

2. Jump

3. Dunk

You'll have to understand all three aspects individually and then understand as well the mechanics of how they all fit together.

Once you're able to accomplish this, you may then add a fourth aspect, which is the ability to do stunts.

But, for now, you should focus on learning the basics first if you're serious about improving your dunking skills.

A dunk necessarily begins with approaching the basket, which can be done in three steps.

Take note that if you dash all the way to the rim, you might make some unnecessary sideways motion that will ultimately make the dunk a bit trickier.

What you need to do is to first master the fundamentals of dunking and then once you have done that, you can start focusing on increasing the speed of your approach.

Make sure you don't finish your approach right beneath the basket, as this can require you to stretch and reach around the edge of the rim, which can make the dunk all the more difficult.

Practice consistency in your approach, as this will help you cultivate your dunking skills more quickly.

The jump is perhaps the key component to a successful dunk.

And the lack of jumping ability may be the number one barrier that's keeping many basketball players from executing a powerful dunk.

The good news is that you can always learn to jump higher.

And the best way to do this is by setting minor objectives first and then working your way up to being able to jump exceptionally high.

Some people are confused as to whether it's best to leap off of just one or both feet.

Well, you can actually jump in whichever manner is most comfortable, or which one allows you to jump higher.

To practice jumping, it may be best to come as near the net as possible without being directly underneath it.

Next, jump up and attempt to reach the rim.

Remember that in order for you to dunk successfully, you'll have to get your wrist on top of the hoop.

Jog around the court for about 15 minutes and then try for the rim again.

You may also want to follow a vertical hop training course to increase your jump height.

Once you're able to get the ball higher than the rim, all you will need is to practice your timing and coordination skills so you can finally dunk that basketball in.

This part of the process will be far from effortless, but if you work hard at it, you will surely appreciate the results it can deliver.

In no time at all, you'll be impressing others with your mighty slam dunks.

PART 6
Squats:
The Best Exercise
for Improving Your
Dunking Skills

When you see basketball superstars like Kobe Bryant rushing to the net and then ending their dash with an explosive dunk, you're naturally inspired to learn how to accomplish the same feat, right?

Well, the good news is that you can actually do that.

You just need to perform the right exercises to strengthen your leg and core muscles such that you can leap higher and be better able to dunk that basketball powerfully into the net.

Remember, though, that learning how to dunk require a lot of determination and an unshakeable will to work on your skills even when you don't really feel like practicing or working out.

Among the most important things you need to learn is that the Squat is the main exercise for improving your vertical leap.

What makes this exercise so special?

Well, for one thing, squats deliver a lot of benefits when they're done with proper form.

This exercise targets your quads, calves, hamstrings, and your gluteus maximus.

Needless to say, all of these muscles play huge roles when you make a leap, which is why it's important to strengthen them.

Aside from strengthening your main leg muscles, squats also trigger the release of growth hormones in your body, which means that it helps you gain overall strength as well when done correctly.

However, squats can lead to some serious injuries when you do them with poor form, which is why you have to be very careful in performing them.

There are lots of common mistakes people make when doing squats, and these mistakes keep them from taking full advantage of the exercise in their efforts to increase jump height.

Arching your back is among the most common mistakes people make when doing a squat.

Not only does this mistake keep you from reaping the benefits of a squat, but it can also lead to back injury over time.

When you squat with the barbell resting on your upper back, you should avoid rolling your lower back, as this can also lead to back problems over time.

Doing squats with your head down is also another common mistake a lot of athletes are guilty of.

Take note that when you look down, you're most likely not keeping your back straight, and keeping the back straight is indeed very important for doing squats in proper form.

People commonly bring their knees in when they perform squats.

The problem is that you are distributing the weight on your body when you do this, and that is a form of cheating where squats are concerned.

Remember that squats should work all of your major muscle groups such as your calves, hamstrings, and quadriceps to ensure that you're reaping its full benefits.

The squat is indeed a great exercise for increasing your jump height.

And the fact that it delivers a host of other benefits makes it even more ideal.

As long as you perform it correctly, you will surely appreciate all the gains you get from this exercise not only for basketball, but for your overall health as well.

PART 7
Shooting Skills You Can't Do Without

To enhance your skills in basketball, you'll most definitely need to develop some specific skills.

Needless to say, shooting the ball with accuracy is among the most important skills you need to learn.

This is especially true if you're currently not scoring points on a significant number of shots that you make.

Of course, effective ball handling and good defense are also essential parts of becoming a good basketball player, but exceptional shooting skills are a must for you to score the necessary points for your team to win.

To enhance your basketball shooting skills, you need to use proper form.

Now, you might get a little confused as to what exactly is proper form because this has been debated by players and coaches alike over the years.

There are shooting forms that have been taught from the early years of the sport and there are also variations that have been recently developed by some players.

Perhaps the best option for you is to learn the basic mechanics of shooting the basketball and then build on those skills as you get more game experience.

There are, of course, some general pointers you can follow in your efforts to enhance your shooting skills.

For instance, when holding the ball in your shooting hand, make sure that you hold it far enough in your hand such that your wrist bends back.

Shoot the ball by pushing it toward the hoop with your hand directly behind it.

To ensure proper form, your arm should follow through after you release the ball.

A good follow through involves letting your arm extend outward and your wrist flop downward.

If you are executing a jump shot, try to land in the same spot where you leapt from as much as possible.

Focusing on landing on the same spot will help improve your balance and accuracy, which is important for taking successful shots.

Take note, however, that landing on the same spot isn't always possible when you're on the run or when a defender is moving in on you.

What's important is that you do your best to make that shot as well-balanced and as accurately as you can.

As much as being able to make shots accurately is important to scoring, it is equally important to be able to make those shots while you're under pressure from a defensive player.

Remember that the opposing team will do everything they can to stop you from making that shot.

Therefore, you should avoid being forced to make bad shots as much as possible.

In the same way, you should also avoid making ball handling mistakes as you take a shot against a defender.

Being able to make a quick release will help you avoid getting too much pressure from the defense.

A good way of practicing your skills in quickly releasing the ball, while still making accurate shots is to position some balls at different points on the court.

Ask someone to time you and then shoot one ball after the other, making sure you keep proper form, but moving at a faster pace than usual.

As you gradually increase your speed and keep your accuracy, you'll start building your confidence in your shots as well.

In due time, you'll be better able to take even the most difficult shots with the greatest amount of pressure, and your shooting and scoring percentages will begin to rise.

This, in turn, will increase your value to the team and make you a basketball player truly worth keeping.

PART 8
Shooting Drills

There are several skills you need to learn in basketball, and all of these skills are definitely needed for your team to win in a basketball game.

However, accurate shooting is what will ultimately give you the scores needed for a win.

Simply put, the more shots your team can make in a game, the more likely you are to win that game.

In fact, a team with good shooting stats is considered a great threat by their opponents because their players will have to be guarded very tightly, which can be very exhausting for the defenders.

For any serious basketball player, there's no better sound than the swish of a ball going through the net.

So, if you want to hear this sound more often, then you'll definitely need to improve on your shooting skills.

Remember that the primary purpose of a basketball game is to shoot the ball through the hoop.

In doing this, it's very important for you to maintain proper form, exhibit good timing, and follow through with your shots.

There isn't a hard and fast rule as regards the proper shooting form, but what's important is for the ball to feel comfortable leaving your shooting hand.

The good news is that there are lots of shooting drills that can help you improve on your basketball shooting skills.

These drills are all about helping you shoot the ball with good form and release the ball comfortably each time you take a shot.

In general, good form requires the ball to be held by your fingertips, your elbows tucked in, an up-and-out shooting direction, and a follow through with good backspin.

Furthermore, shooting drills help increase your ability to shoot the ball accurately from all angles, positions, and distances on the court.

When you shoot from a short distance, you'll definitely need a good, solid shooting form.

This is, in fact, the key element in being a good shooter.

The form shooting drill can be very useful in enhancing your skills in short distance shooting.

Specifically, this drill allows you to develop good and solid shooting form by using a relatively close basket range.

The drill is performed by standing about three feet from the backboard on one side of the basket.

Make a shot from this position, making sure you keep proper form.

You'll then need to rebound the ball and then make the same shot again.

You'll need to make 15 shots on each side, shooting with your right hand on the right side of the basket and with your left hand on the left side.

Once you've made all shots on both sides, move three feet farther from the basket and then repeat the drill.

To improve your long distance accuracy, you would do well to do distance shooting drills as well.

After all, becoming a better offensive player requires you to have exceptional long distance shooting skills.

No matter how you good you may feel when you dunk the ball right into the hoop, it's still a lot more exciting to knock down a three-pointer, especially during a crucial game.

Therefore, if you want to be known for your shooting abilities, then you'll definitely have to work on extending your shooting range.

And distance shooting drills, when done correctly and regularly, is a very good way to extend your range.

Distance shooting drill is done by first shooting at a distance you're comfortable with.

Take about ten shots, aiming for at least 80% shooting percentage.

Once you're able to achieve an 80% shooting percentage at this range, you'll have to move back a foot or two farther and then repeat the drill.

Continue moving farther back as you hit an 80% shooting percentage with each set of shots.

Remember to keep proper form while shooting, regardless of the distance.

You can stop moving back when you can no longer shoot with proper form.

Remember that shooting is the key basketball skill you need to master if you want to be a good player and if you want to help carry your team to big wins.

Therefore, basic shooting drills should always be part of your regular basketball training routine.

As you master these drills and improve your shooting accuracy at different angles and distances, you'll also grow more confident in your overall basketball skills.

PART 9
How to Score
Without the Ball

Unless you're playing the point-guard position, it's safe to say that you won't have the ball for about four-fifths of the time you spend on the court.

This may come as a surprise, but moving without the ball is also an essential skill you need to master in basketball.

In fact, scouts usually look for such a skill in players because it tells them that you've got high basketball IQ and that you're able to make use of all available space on the court.

This skill also shows that you've got different sides to your game, and it thereby takes you to the next level, getting you closer to your dream of becoming an unstoppable scorer on the basketball court.

There are lots of ways for you to move without the ball such that you create space for easy scoring.

The good news is that these techniques are not very difficult to master.

Cuts and give and goes are just two of the best ways to create space and get into scoring position even when you don't have the ball.

And you would surely appreciate the fact that improving your skills at moving without the ball can easily add eight or more points to your game.

Give and Go

This technique is done with a reverse V cut.

When you have the ball in your hands, you'll have to dribble and then pass it to one of your teammates.

You should then take a couple of steps in the direction of the pass and then cut back in the opposite direction.

Move towards the hoop, prepared to take the return pass and make that all-important shot.

V Cut
This move is perhaps the easiest move to perfect.

The idea is to fake moving towards the rim.

As you get close to the rim, stop and make a sudden sharp movement towards the ball.

When you pair this move with a quick release of the ball, it can be a good source of high-percentage shots.

Back Cut
Also known as the backdoor cut, this move is especially effective for use against a persistent defender who tries to deny you the ball by staying as close to you as possible.

You do this by moving towards the ball and then suddenly pushing up your front foot and moving back towards the basket.

This move will most likely have you ending up with a nice layup or even a dunk.

L Cut
This is a must-have for any basketball scorer, since it gives you the option of either driving to the hoop for a layup or to get up a shot.

This move is especially effective when your defender isn't too close.

It requires you to move quickly in one direction and then let out a burst of speed in the opposite direction.

This should effectively lose your defender and give you the perfect chance to make a good shot.

Curl

This move is done with one of your teammates screening you.

As the scorer, you need to be aware of the screen while masking this awareness from your defender.

You can do this effectively by moving away from the screen such that your drag the defender away with you.

Then, in a sharp turn, move quickly towards the screen and go around it to get to the ball.

This move guarantees a high-percentage shot all the time.

PART 10
Strength Training? The Best Way to Enhance Your Skills

You may have noticed that there's a lot of debate going on about which basketball workout truly delivers the greatest gains, particularly for improving vertical jumps.

Is it plyometric training or strength training?

Now, what makes the issue even more confusing is that some people even espouse a combination of these two workouts as the best option for enhancing your basketball skills.

The reason why it can be quite difficult to decide which workout works best for you is the fact that every person is built differently.

The truth is that there can be very little difference in the results you gain from plyometric training and strength training where vertical jump improvement is concerned.

This is especially true during the first month or two of training.

Perhaps the most important thing you need to remember is that when you're training for basketball, your vertical jump has to be both quick and explosive.

Now, if you're able to squat perfectly with heavy weights in the gym, but aren't quite achieving the vertical jumps that should go with your weight lifting achievements, then perhaps it's time to try plyometric training and see if you'll get better gains.

Plyometrics is equally important if you feel that you're a naturally springy person, but you still struggle in the gym with your squats, dead lifts, and other leg workouts.

Plyometric training teaches your muscles to contract quickly as a response to loading.

To understand plyometrics better, always remember that strength and power are two different things.

Where strength is simply the ability to deliver force, power refers to the ability to deliver that force over a certain period of time.

In achieving a high vertical jump, it's important for your muscles to not only contract forcefully, but also to contract quickly.

Of course, this isn't to say that strength training isn't important.

On the contrary, strength training may be the necessary first step to improving your jumping skills in basketball.

Look at strength training as the engine that powers your jump and plyometrics as the electronics that help deliver the necessary power to the wheels, which are your legs in this case.

All things considered, a combination of strength training and plyometrics may really be the best option for you in terms of improving your basketball skills.

It's a given fact that basketball players spend hours at the gym trying to improve their overall physical strength.

Therefore, improving your game in basketball simply means making adjustments to incorporate plyometrics into your training, and possibly doing more compound exercises like squats and dead lifts.

The good news is that doing a combination of strength training and plyometrics can be applied both by men and women.

Furthermore, you can successfully apply them regardless of your fitness category and basketball experience.

Whether you're a pick-up game warrior or a professional athlete, you'll surely benefit from these two basketball workouts.

Just remember to measure your results after about ten weeks, as measuring too quickly can make you feel as if you're not getting anywhere.

Take note that gains are steady, although they may not appear in big bursts.

PART 11
Basketball and VO2max

Did you know that there is a young basketball player who is not only doing amazingly well on the basketball court, but is also a great track star?

In fact, this player was already breaking records in both sports even at the very young age of eleven.

When tests were conducted on this boy, doctors found that he had extremely high levels of VO2max in his body.

For you to make significant improvements in your own game, you would do well to gain a better understanding of exactly what VO2max is and what it has to do with the kid's amazing prowess in sports.

VO2max is the maximum capacity of your body to transport and use oxygen during exercise, which reflects your overall physical fitness.

You don't have to learn all about the actual measurement of VO2max in your body, as that is all math and science, and doesn't really help you play basketball better anyway.

What you need to know is why VO2max is important.

To put it simply, VO2max is the amount of oxygen your body takes in whenever you exert yourself.

It is determined when your consumption of oxygen remains at a steady rate despite an increase in workload.

Doctors and other experts agree that the measurement of VO2max is the single best determining factor of a person's cardiovascular fitness and maximal aerobic power.

The reason for this is that it takes oxygen for you to breathe while exercising, and exercise is still the best way to strengthen muscles like your heart.

Endurance training has been found to be most effective at increasing your VO2max levels.

What made the 11-year-old boy exceptional in sports is the fact that his VO2max level is that of a 20-year-old marathon runner.

This means he doesn't reach that out-of-breath feeling as quickly as other boys his age do.

In fact, he doesn't reach that level as quickly as many adult athletes do.

Part of what makes his VO2max level so high is his dedication to sports training, and the good news for him is that this will continue to increase as long as he keeps up with the same kind of dedicated training.

You, too, can benefit from high VO2max levels if you start working as hard as this kid does.

Aerobic power is especially important to basketball players like you, since the game itself requires a lot of intense activity throughout the game's duration.

It's equally important for you to realize that VO2max tests have been regularly used in combination with other indicators to determine the aerobic power and general physiological condition of athletes undergoing basketball skills training.

Although levels of VO2max can sometimes be characterized by genetics, it can also be improved through appropriate endurance training.

The French physiologist Veronique Billat has created the 30/30 and the 60/60 interval technique specifically to help you improve your VO2max levels.

This technique requires you to warm up for about ten minutes, run as fast as you can for about 30 seconds, and then move to a steady jogging pace for another 30 seconds.

Continue with these 30/30 intervals for at least 12 times, after which you may move on to 60/60 interval training.

As your VO2max levels rise, you can expect your explosive power on the basketball court to improve as well.

In fact, raising VO2max levels may be a very important part of basketball skills training for young and adult players alike.

Once you've achieved your optimum VO2max levels, you can truly take competitive advantage over your opponents, as you're less likely to tire out and can therefore out-perform the other players.

PART 12
Why Some People Don't Play Basketball

Ask any basketball enthusiast and they'll all tell you that basketball is more than just a game.

It is, in fact, a lifestyle.

But, if enthusiasts truly feel this way, why do many of them refuse to play the game and are instead content to watch from the sidelines and cheer their favourite players on?

If you're one of these people who don't dare to play, but somehow wish you could, then you should gain a better understanding of what usually hinders people from playing basketball.

Understanding the hindrances is the necessary first step towards overcoming them and finally being able to play the game you so love.

Inconsistency
Most people find it very difficult to be consistent.

The problem is that basketball requires a great deal of consistency in order to attain success.

Performing the necessary drills for just a few days at a time just won't cut it.

Remember that repetition is the key to training your body to do things in a certain way.

If you're not willing to make the type of effort needed to become the player that you dream of becoming, then you'll never achieve your dream of becoming a professional athlete.

Lack of Hard Work

Are you willing to work as hard as you possibly can in order to improve your basketball skills?

You may have a lot of natural talent, but you may not be willing to work as hard as necessary, which may be why you can't play basketball at the level you'd like to play.

Playing basketball requires you to practice regularly, even if nobody asks you to and even if nobody else is around.

You should never take your natural talent for granted.

Your unwillingness to work hard is the major hindrance you'll have to overcome so you can be a great basketball player.

Goal-setting

Many people are satisfied with watching rather than playing because they don't want to go through the process of setting goals.

Visualizing the end even before you begin is essential for attaining success in basketball.

It encourages you to do whatever it takes to make that vision a reality.

Now, if you really want to become a good basketball player, your primary goal should be to work hard on your skills every single day.

Mental Toughness

This is another value you need to possess if you want to start playing basketball.

Take note that basketball can be a very shaky business, meaning nobody plays well every single time.

If you're not mentally tough enough to handle instances when you're playing a bad game, then you'll most likely stop playing altogether.

You have to learn how to deal with such disappointments and rise up from a bad game to do better the next time.

Choosing Your Peers

The kind of people you hang around with can have a huge effect on your decision to give your dream a go or not.

If you hang around people who don't really take basketball seriously, then that kind of attitude is likely to rub off on you.

On the other hand, hanging out with people who are constantly working to improve their game will also inspire you to do the same.

So, if you're really interested in learning how to play basketball and play it well, then you'd best surround yourself with people who play the game as well.

Remember that hindrances can only hold you back if you let them.

Basketball is meant to be played, especially by those who aspire to be great at it.

So, leave all the negativity behind and start setting your goals and then working hard to achieve them.

Printed in Poland
by Amazon Fulfillment
Poland Sp. z o.o., Wrocław